THE
CASKETMAKER

For Jane & Donald
From Ron
w/ all best.
Aug. 9-85

——THE——
CASKETMAKER

Selected
Shorter
Poems
1960-1970

by Ronald H. Bayes

JOHN F. BLAIR, *Publisher*
Winston-Salem, North Carolina

—To—

Frederick Candelaria
Gerald Jones
Harry Meacham
W. D. White

G.A.H.C!

ACKNOWLEDGMENTS

The author wishes to express appreciation to the following publications for permission to reprint poems previously published in their pages:
South & West, The Middle R, Subterraneans (Tokyo), *The Reporter* (Portland), *The Scandinavian Review, The Yale Literary Magazine, In/sert, Emphasis Oregon, Poetry Pendulum, National Poetry Anthology, Etchings, Human Voice Quarterly, Grande Ronde Review, Poems of 1961* (England), *Dunklin City Press, Wormwood Review, Trace, Palimpsest, Elizabeth, Jeopardy, Poetry Parade, Penny Poems of Amarillo College, University of Portland Review, December, West Coast Review, Voices International, South Florida Poetry Journal, Southern Poetry Review, Novakast Press* (Tokyo), *Poetry Nippon, Symposium Poets* (Defiance College), *Blitz, Poems from the Pacific Northwest Poetry Conference* (Reed College, 1966), *Pembroke Magazine,* and *Camels Coming.*

The author is also grateful to the Harvard University Press for permission to quote from *The Odes* by Ezra Pound.

CONTENTS

I form a casket here
to hold secure
all precious things
and memories and dreams.

N. H. Leif, "Persons"

Here, catch this casket; it is
worth the pains.

Shakespeare, *The Merchant*
of Venice, II, VI

—I—

Parallels

THE CASKETMAKER

Because it pleases me I turn to you
this lightless hour, and ask a reassurance
that cannot be there, although you touch me
and respect a smile of which I'm half ashamed.

The time is mine and selfishly I share
the sudden flash, sheet lightning of my
mind, unapt to start a fire or cause a
rain, denote direction sure enough to take;

And you can see my clutching—like a sea
anemone poked with a stick, neither in defense
nor sure aggression out of will: I build,
I drive, I turn to you again. Admire the nail.

RECOLLECT
(for Don Ludwigsen in Alaska)

Gaffs
of time got us
through the gills.

Your black cat
your only crew you
handle your craft asea.

I grasp your hand,
hooker for a salmon, or
five thousand.

I bump in the air
headed for Los Angeles
wishing to

See waters off Ketchikan,
in spite of vertigo
be on fjords again.

3

FOR A FRIEND WHO WALKED GIRDERS

I fumble at the weaving of a garland for you
with whom a certain grace
of understanding came late,
at the right time, out of place.
Regardless of the calendar
the fumble-fingered man I was
and am; note how the things
pop out of place in eye, in fact—
but string and color, stalk and
vine of mine I wind, now, briefly
together for you, in grief,
this way, for at least one last time
and at least one first.

That I have never seen a finer
love than yours, or hurt more deep
makes me confess the mystery.
And now I think illogically about
your summer with the bridges,
rivets caught death-high, in air,
knowing time lines extend some things.
Some things stand out because
they should,
because they must.

Eyes sometimes come alive in paintings
where there are only almond whites,
clocks stop when the dead love
or want to touch us; when the dead love
the living and when we reciprocate.
And sometimes through such doors
in spite of our desire, loved ones
insist on entering. Then we can only
touch and hope; make hope a garland,
hope touch will suffice and we can
—will be allowed to—take
a world at a time.

ONCE AGAIN ON THAT THEME FROM CATULLUS
(for Rolfe Humphries)

Odi et amo quare id faciam
    fortasse requiris?
Nescio. Sed fieri sentio ac
    excrucior.

I hate; I love.
You ask me why.
I do not know
although I try
to understand:
And I must cry
"It pains! it chokes!
in life I die!"

IN DUMBARTON

1.

In Dumbarton
the little girl
pirouetted in the archway
with the cat.
Swans in a flock appeared to me
a dingy lot, in Ayr:
I could code no meaning there,
nor in the presence of
Dumbarton Rock,
or all of Long, the loch itself,
thinking on the sheep
swollen and dead at Nardwick,
the laugh of touring girls
together in summer London,
and two puny Dublin girls in the after hours
hole—
the Medoc there,
its bitterness
and ten bob lent a stranger:
How focus almost came steady near Bayswater Road
with the old man's hand of friendship
(seventy, desperate, but full of pluck—
all plastic from the Blitz, the civil service,
and a teaching turnout, earlier);

he'd no idea he spat breadcrumbs on me
with the enthusiastic verbs;
I didn't mind.

Think and thought on the too-possessive,
sad Scots orphan headed for the Volunteers—
"I have no friends,
just know them I work with,"
        toothless, hopeless smile,
scared, seventeen, duck-heading into life.

And two dear cows stood
at evening
head to head,
stubborn and chewing
in a good and peaceful *is*.

Our bus raced for Kilmarnock.

2.

Frank Pond, blind, went far
but poor, selling songs—
New York to Walla Walla to Miami;
didn't have a dog to guide him.

3.

Six years ago when I went home
a new and mongrel pup tore down
a clothesline;
stole wash cloths, towels, and
                    underdrawers,
home, there at Umapine.
   We laughed together, you and I,
so scolded, with no mind to punish
that exuberance.
      When I remarked
"Dog giveth and dog takes away,"
you laughed again and said "It's sinful,
but what I was thinking."

God, *means* are funny things!
And *ends*?
. . . They always need tied up,
but have fast legs.

POEM TO A SOLDIER: BASE LIBRARY

Putting sex drive into squeaking shoe sides,
ankles crossing under the crude, brown table,
khaki-clad, he writes his letter—
aiming, straining cold miles out from home's love.

Warmth is intense as crinkling sheets are fumbled;
now come fiercer, faster leather screeches.
Cockeyed, purple stamps set passion solid;
Xes tattoo flap when tonguing's ended.

I pause the moment, irked by this young fool,
recalling higher loves book-learned at school,
pity a little—envy more; I think:
what's to be won in act, and what in ink?

SPRING IN ICELAND
(Near Sangerdi: May)

To Iceland?
To Iceland
Spring comes slowly
late in the solstice,
greening the grass
and keening the spirit.

Late in May's weeks a
reprieve from
some seawinds
and stay from
the stabs of
snow seeking the shalerock.

The light comes
to Iceland
longing with windwhip,
then lolls the tired heart,
warms as the mind moves
passion sustained
long as forevers
promised by lovers.

In May now
—in green stuff
and this place—
forget the Winter.

ROAD SCENE:
KEFLAVIK TO HAFNAFJORDUR

Pillarclouds
and a plane
and the plane does not belong;
even sheep wool on the fence
is out of place.
Tedious, the plain-wood church
paralleling spire to door,
a mock security, secures more
through white paint.

It looks like four-bottomed Bunion-plows
went through the lava here;
northward the stacked rock guides the way for ghosts,
and west—cold lava far as eye can see
stretching into distance, dark.
  The bay by Keflavik today's
  whelped blue as new sky!

Gunnar, turned back to green, in his way
burnt—not quite like Njal.
Often we turn back, lots of us.
Remark those houses, walls, lava, knolls,
sea, rock, and cloud;
note the white walls and houses in pastels,
but most the
green, green, green.

FROM AN ICELAND PASTURE RANGE

1. (*By a Fjord*)

One whistle on the wind;
less than a second, gone.

2. (*Dead Sheep*)

The sheep is dead
in the middle
of the pasture range
(rock and green mottle).
The manly boy kicks his head,
crunches a horn down with an iron prod,
carefully,
says
"Wake up! The flock left here
a damn long time ago!"
and laughs harshly.
Instantly silence
absorbs his laugh.

THE PHILADELPHIA AIRPORT

Rather tired at the Philadelphia airport.
And the plane to board
an hour and three coffees away.

What irony that at five-thirty A.M.
I am at last moved by emotion
(it has been a long time) when
the unavoidable, continual soft-music loudspeaker
romps a certain German polka,

And I remember another airport,
other years,
and I who have never wished to go back before
wish to go back.
But one never can in time
(and does space matter much?).
Want some irony?
In Germany it was—you weren't there—
and I loved you: Christ! with what passion
of intensity; jealous of whomever you were with

With the dawn pink and blue and grey and
the trees mushroom clumping
like wanting Breughel
to red-in country rompers—or
maybe someone good at satyrs—

And I remember that other airport,
I remember a polka
and that I loved you.

Now each in maze muddled and adjusting
and we no longer love. Why kid? And I am not
even jealous in wild imaginings.

A few people,
a few more people:
now we move . . . you move . . . I move . . . from progress
to progress,
unlove to unlove,
anticipating only departures.

I THINK ON HAWKS' HEARTS
AS YOU WALK THE BEACH

Before the cockspurs of the world gouged your eyes,
that bloodied birdbeak of torn lips smiled once
of love all red, then came the cold, thin line
like ice biting protection's brassy bit,
you were, I think, a lovely dove and calm.

After the condor lusts had hurled your heart away,
not comprehended and less understood
a fester nurtured in the green of *if*
moved for the good. Still earth's mourning
set your singing's only tone and struck your keys.

Before the pain of *why*, but after *is*, I knew
your contradictions, touch and thinking too,
all ripe as hate and red as were spur thrusts
—yet calling "life" and calling "yes" to me.
But still the bit and still the icy line.

And yet you were, I swear, a dove—once on a time.

OFF ST. GEORGE'S BAY
(Bermuda: April)

Quiet but for humming
of an ocean-going tug
somewhere near.
   A mile of azure motion
   calm as lotus.
Lovely under a Bright growing excited flowers
St. George's is warm, too, with white, pink-washed
cottages: coral-cut, half-mile across the sound they
glitter and flower above where
the still *Arosa Star* stays docked.

And the water skiers not yet at their play,
nor swimmers
—it's a little chilly in, a little bit too early.
This is the selfish, glorious, secret time
for the lone looker
to lave in beauty
and love the stillness,
lording it on his own,
knowing the need to believe in some good
not quite out of this moment;
having it filled.

LYDETTE

Gay and garlanded
down to the dockside
my love came running.

Warm that welcoming
by azure waters,
and both of us laughing.

So shall I love her,
hearing her laughter
at each journey's end,

Never forgetting my
smiling and flowered,
my dear love, running.

GOING SOUTH

They'd made the start from North Washington,
passed through Walla Walla,
Milton-Freewater,
I joining there the busload,
and God but they were without.

So little!
Blankets and baskets and the Greyhound creaking
baskets and blankets and a cardboard box
glasses and rubber boots
knotted brown hands
and everything and hope on board, in short.

Up and down hills:
Weston, Athena, Pendleton,
And I recall somewhere between he looked at her,
turning half-round his seventy-wintered and rheumatic head
and thrilling spastic-like, jerking words because of
February cold,
to California-or-bust, his partner, wife, said,
"Mother, I can feel it. It's getting warmer
already,"
said, "We're in Oregon now, you know.
It's quite a difference."

I couldn't wince,
nor could I choose to ponder on the heart's brown moment
with twelve above outside and cold feet, too.

I knew it wasn't really getting warmer,
mountains ahead and open land with gusts of wind soon up
the Columbia River Gorge to the right; the Bend
southmountain country ditto.

"My God!" I said inside
"How can they keep this poor act up—
this poor pretense at hope."
But they had to and they knew and I knew and I wanted
    with them,
wanted with them,
but knew it wasn't getting any warmer,
except, perhaps,
the region of the heart.

PARALLELS: UMAPINE
(for E. P.)

Dingdongs the broken
hollyhock.
From stem atop
red flowers
in afternoon's warm
early hours, swing,
spent. Bloomings
continue round-about
abject defeat and side by,
lush as decay,
stay without seeing
early August's breeze
competing with the blizzard—
ah, devastation too is relative—
tidal wave, typhoon.

VOICES FOR GRANDFATHER'S MEMORY

"Roll your tails and roll 'em high
We'll all be angels, bye and bye."
(which he liked to sing to the cows
herding them in, some milking times)

Father or God
pain or sleep,
and dog with questioning eye
uplifted.

Never admit when you are bested.

That that is is that requested.

Lilt and love
the Eden days
and yellow pumpkin;
tractor and lane
and the clean dust.

Fly in the waterjug
how long ago that August day
I dumped it all and somehow he
held that temper in check.

Shocked on that day we suddenly
knew our time to be together was short.

Then October:
the boy by the bed
in tears through tears
wanting an answer

Turned the crank,

So loved and hurt,

Moved towards a man.

Plan by hope—but life by fight.

Up by Is.

And the fence went down.

Chase the cows
one last time
in.

Lose the dare,
but God-damn Death!

2.

Into the dark night
he went by day,
hated and loved,
and wracked with pain.

Grey of hair and keened by hurt.

Rheumy of eye from recurrent thought.

Reft of hope
but full of "will be."
Father and warrior finally said
"This is enough."

"Hell is now and Heaven plenty."

I think pasture, greening,
heard my heart weep
when I buried my face in the brown cow's side
and wetted her hair with tears.

> Father and God.
> Pain and sleep.
> Dog with innocent eye
> unquestioned.
> Never admit when you are bested.
> That is all that is requested.
>
> Lilt and love the Eden days,
> the hay-rake days; pumpkin time
> and frequent pheasant;
> tractor and land
> and the clean dust.
> This is enough.

CHAPTER

At evening on your farm
did you ever put eggs in your pockets,
see if you could do what others had
screwed up at? You know, they busted them
once some kid, Dad said?

One time I got brave enough to, scared at that,
because my Aunt Exa was there;
and I found this nest by the ditch
and put two in each pocket and
ran like hell.   They busted.

And boy it was gooey, and it was slick
and I felt sick
and I knew, boy I knew I'd goofed.
But nobody scolded—since Exa was there.

Who's sorry he tried running?

FOR JORGEN KRUHOFFER
(At Sondrestrom, Greenland)

The old man
who young
took the same trip
each day
into the Japanese garden
down the shaded path
to the lake
to have talk with the golden-scaled fish
on important questions
leads me
leads me
land to land to land.
And to each far lake we go
to glimpse ripple,
gilt flash against blue,
to fathom the whole if we may have a word.

And I watch his palsied head,
untiring eyes,
that withered, pointing hand,
always
my only companions
land to land.

HAVE YOU EVER SEEN?

Have you ever seen a real beautiful
hurt
bird
that looked calm, possessed, unruffled,
so that the wound surprised you
when you found it somehow though you knew
it would not stay still unless it had to?
—And feeling it the wound hurt you
and you wisht you could somehow
take it from the bird,
for which already you had the feeling—love,
and tears at the ready at the ready
on the quick assembly line.
And you knew that its dying
or its getting well would free the bird:
Away flying
would be the last you'd love of that, see.

But you can't just

VARIATION ON A THEME
BY ROLFE HUMPHRIES

The misinterpretation is what hurts.
"The last collapse surprises most,"
as Humphries said.

Perhaps the reasoning was bad at first:
we know that all communication
is impure, some way.

Perhaps the terms were ill advised,
perhaps we changed the aim unknowingly—
and all communication is

Impure some way. Impure some way:
always we kid ourselves so cunningly
collapses shock.

Especially the last.

—II—

*Certain Times,
Certain Lines*

PAN: SECOND SIGHT

Pan the camera
    you
    by the sun-dial,
    half tame,
and why not? It is
    hot
and your skin
has the texture, the sheen
that caused somebody
    (and your hair)
to invent
I think
kodachrome.

"One and the same."

The concrete god
remembers
too.

RECONSIDERATION

The lover of
that other summer
came to visit me.
> 'Can't we resume? at
> least a while?'

Now what retort
can you make
to a thing
like that?

And outside the sun
is high . . .
air right cushion
for a joyous cry.

NONSEASONAL

Passing
how talk about
the full heart the
tears
of emotion
upsurge
of
and toward   (passing)
undefinables in, as Merrill
said, an age of quantification,
hurry,
and I have . . . "and I . . . I . . . I."

Maudlin, then call
these hopes (homely) of
felicitas, puritas, humanitas
need thru
to music of the precise
word, chord, kiss, touch, coloration.
Correlation.
How talk about, as into or out of
blending?

It is here,
even here
the oasis is
this single tree.

HOMAGE TO EMILY DICKINSON, ET AL

The gesture is beyond
me;
coal oil, the lamp has guttered
out.
By day I see the chimney
scorched;
that proves there was heat, some
light;
the gesture never has come
off
with me, time past I mean
they
used to gird up loins,
I tie my shoe.

CHILD OUTSIDE MY WINDOW

The child outside my window howls;
crying is so like laughter—
the child outside my window attests this
and shifts as quickly to my
bachelor ear as geared machinery.
  At first, compassion.
Then, by God, I'm irked;
  this stupid inconsistency!
He should be jerked quite harshly
upright by his careless mother!

Yet I stay still, and then
one half-formed thought sneaks past
of how fast loves pass by,
and then no choice but weep,
soon or at last, be lost or caught.
  The noisy, inconsistent child
outside my window vouches,
shifting so irksome, fast
these intonations.

DEFENDER OF THE FAITH
(Fort Carson)

Said the 17-year-old soldier
to a crowd of three
openmouthed U-kiah farm boys
sittin'
in the guardhouse betwixt postwalkin's
(he from ruddy Montana),
    "Whin ah git home,
ah'm gunna lay
all day long . . .
        an mah wahf'll moover
        laigs like this
        !"

"Nah'll say whin she wantsta
moove,
'Stay hyer nah'll makea boy
t'nite!' . . .
        But ah'll fool her
        (yew know haow)
        kuz ah kaint afford
        inny kids yit."

THE BEACH AT WALDPORT

I think of Cuchulain and
of Arnold on this beach
altogether after and somewhere

between the pebbles and the waves:
some passions, hopes and epic
thrusts and mild coups and humming

lusts are what I wish sustained,
personally. Let the others
shout out their defeats;

I'll watch mine reel back
over the corpse which killed them
and chide Cuchulain, Arnold.

But knock it for lunch:
here she comes calling from the
motel, glass in hand my

lovely in her long stretchpants.
A second glass, looking,
having found me, she hands it.

"Hi, Seriousness!" (She's literate!)
The dirty cap with buckets
and agates. The college studs

eye us as we walk back—her back.
So we repair for nourishment.

FOUR-YEAR-OLD

Teddy bear
and a stick
behind clump-weed and wild rye
he charges the evils of
the world.

O ABOUT IT
(for Bill and Dorothy Stafford)

On the signing of letters it can be said
that where I come from we
all sign our letters
"love"
because failing
like who doesn't
we try to nevertheless to.

BUT TO TELL THE TRUTH

As for flavor
it's hard to best
a rib
said my butcher to
me,
and I thought about
Eve.

SONG FOR SUSAN R.

Huddle, protect the dream,
though the song's lost;

Strangle the swine that killed
the downy bird:

We'll use his bones and
have percussion yet.

THE GOVERNING

"Hello, Puke!"
shouted the former Speaker
of the House

to the
former
Governor

in the capitol, hailing
him hearty,
just before dinner.

MAINLINE MAYDAY

And now the day the pole is
danced about;
see Bryn Mawr maids as one
cavort and shout!
throw posies, coyly wiggle
cultured hips
hot for the haystack,
phallus, sperm, and
blue, blue chips.

LINES FOR THE TIME

I said to
     my barber
"I am trying to
grow bald
       gracefully,"
and he said
"There ain't no such thing."

    And I said
    "I know it
but I want to try *ANYWAY*
and that is what makes
Democracy great."
"Yeh," he said
"So I *SHALL* leave it long
on top,
Mr. Jefferson."

ONE TO GET READY
AND TWO FOR TENURE
(for Hamilton C. Horton, Jr.)

1. (*Liver of Life*)

In the room the professor comes and goes
talking high drama, teen-age prose. But
let us go then, thee and me,
when the system cries "martini,"
not "hot tea."
Let us go through certain sweaty-smelling halls
to lands where, huge and green, the olive falls—
falls aplunking into Seagram's Golden Gin,
and the man who plunks it always wears a grin,
and leave forever genius and the question
whether books reviewed by freshmen bear suggestion
that could lead, unmethodized, to pregnancy
or a runaway teen-ager on a spree, or a fit
of uncontrolled masturbation that might sap
away the vigor of the nation.

> In the room the bursar comes and goes,
> discussing merit pay and picking nose.

And would it have been worth it, after all,
to have told, yes to have told the bitter truth—
that it's better when it's dry than with Vermouth?

2. (*The Matter Has Been Sufficiently*)

Constipated academicians
upholding MLA traditions,
thrusting ahead through open stack,
probe and research Kerouac,
nevertheless not citing Jack the way he goes,
but, rather, "John."

The art is long.

PALM SUNDAY, 1965
(for Philip)

I sit here listening to the wind, the mind,
Oregon cold in this fourth month,
an hour after watching the street
for half an hour ("Will that car stop?
Will the one I wish to
call? When will I die? What love? What?
                         "What, Love?")
What love will move? April, we live in
the North.
     A jeep drove the length of
three alleys and I returned to Iceland,
always to me the island of longing.
          Now on the wind I return.
This is undoubtedly Spring. I am in Oregon.
Here I live. Easter is six days off.

Whalen is in San Francisco.
The train toots its diesel against
the wind. I have many books to read.
I am sure it is just as lonely
in The Dalles.
Sun pale on Mt. Emily, Northeast, and
light on Table Mountain jabs at
the angles of rain.
The second train is difficult on the wind;
even the bell is failing.

The slice of palm leaf is the color
of the room, lights on and all shades up
this day, and an undramatic man I wouldn't wish
to know faces me from the TV's face;
the set is off.

I suppose we both know pretty well
why the old man I eavesdropped accidentally
last hour limped more coming back
ten minutes after strolling out in the direction
of the post office.
Pines and silver poplars still out of leaf.
Red brick and marble front at the Elks Club,
Adams Avenue pretty quiet,
sick brick at The Wheel; the assertion of each
car keeps up (shape and color).
Wimpys, across the street, is closed Sundays.
Orpheus was off the shelf today
and back again today.
This is undoubtedly Spring. I live in Oregon.
Here I am. Easter is six days off.

A COMPLAINT

Because I come
so far
so fast
so unreciprocally believed—
       so damned impossible—
but so in love
demanding only you,
you give me definition
by omitting,
like ashamed.

SEASONAL

Even if we were but ten
tears apart
we were a heart's whirl
beyond mind's measure:
ten years apart though, too?
Greater, my dear, than by foot,
foot by foot
apart
across three centuries,
across, maybe, ten thousand worlds.

Apart.
Part.
A part.
A part apart.
Part part apart.
Pare a heart.
Pair a heart.
A part pare.
A part core.
Apart pair.
Apart core.
Core a part.
A part.

Core's heart.
Course heart!
(Coarse heart!)
Heart's hart in season;
hart's heart, in season.

Here merely I end—
why, dear one, did you start?

COMMANDS

Go away.
I think I love you.
I have a rock to roll up a hill.
Go away.
I love you.
It is essential.

THE NEWS AT DINNERTIME

"Well I blew on it to put it out,"
said the small boy whose playing with matches
caused that big, red roar—
"blew on it to put it out,
but it didn't do any good."

I TRY TO HEAR WHAT THEY SAID

Turning to me in bed
on New Year's night, you, angry
said "Open your eyes,"
said "You're not making love
to a memory. I'm no abstraction."

Odd, that
I never thought of you
as abstract, until
much later, pondering
and bedding eye to eye.

Then one of us left the
other or we both moved off.
Oh my architect, my aesthetician,
we needed to meet and had to cope
—although we didn't well.

Now I keep my eyes open in bed
and laugh a lot
lust a little, love,
put away thought but always
make it eyeball to eyeball.

—III———————

Considerations,
Translations, and
Constructions

Glorious and abundant
The cherry trees are in flower
In all the world there is nothing
Finer than brotherhood.
            The Odes, E. P.
            translating Kung

KOZA CITY: FEBRUARY

In the hallway
the song
and the foot's rhythm,
your quiet voice
sings flowers and peace;
this love.

How it
is not like myself
to smile
thus,
seeing one I
love loved.

The first cherries
bloom North,
at Nago.
You say
we will look,
we two.

CHEONG

You'll roast
me a pig at
a party; phone me twice
after midnight to say I should
come back;

You'll get
a flat for us
right on the water's edge
in Singapore. For your smile
I'd come back.

PLUM AND APRICOT:
APPLE AND ROSE

Wise in
their way they
left us by ourselves,
that we could hold our hearts,
each the other's,
three dawns.

SHRINE

I.

Neither of us is a good tourist,
still, very tired
on the first day of the New Year
we went to the
Temple of the Emerald Buddha
together, who had
had love a day and a half.
And the New Year, bright,
seemed frightening and proper.
We each bought Lord Buddha
some small flowers;
we did not even whisper
when we removed our shoes,
nor when we knelt in the crowd.
  The deep beauty of that place
was beyond the saying,
and your going right to the foot
of the Lord Buddha
to offer the flowers, though I,
afraid, left mine on the floor,
though wanting to be in your heart
as sure and deep as
Lord Buddha's stone is set in.

And you left to meditate,
I stayed to meditate.
We met later in the crowd
outside the gate, glaze-eyed and
directionless in the traffic.

II.

Now we are these miles
away, readied for
another parting,
words in our way
as ever they've been.

Tokyo is bright in the sun
but the wind is coming up.
You are two hours away—
and tomorrow, which seems
a century away, another last time.

There's nothing for it.
I shall climb the hill
to the Shinto Shrine
behind my room and pray,
and clap my hands, softly.

PARTING IN OKINAWA—
AND THE CAMBODIAN DUSK

I.

Two boys
rode out of sunset holding hands
two girls holding hands
twos, more twos
holding hands,
                rode their
bikes
home from school
in Seam Reap
down General deGaulle Avenue
                    holding hands
like hands
ripped off
in war
    a few miles away
on the border;
girls and boys holding hands
             ages
12, 10, 15.

    (Hands not
     severed hands
     take my worship; boys,
     girls like new flowers.)

———————————

And in Phnom Penh
the American jet
shot down
over Cambodian land
　　　　mounted
on a heap of cement,
　　　　　　And my sad hostess:
"Would you like to see
the highway the Americans helped us build
that went
　　　　almost
to the sea?"

II.

This last day together
in Nago
you lean against my shoulder;
"I am very sad," you say.
And I am too.

　　　　　　Tan
tatami,
the single flower
in the house's place of honor
and a lovesong on the television from Tokyo.
Your Mama smiles

57

and pours beer
after such a fine meal,

                     our last together.
Yoshiko is like a flower, her hands
folded, smiling to see
we are such brothers.

I am very sad.

————————————

    Distressed, too, at the island's
insane, new inflation, and that
American officialdom

                has caused
as much of it as have greedy

                   Okinawan capitalists
and bureaucrats.

              And I worry
that in days ahead
this will keep

          the likes of us
apart,
harden and cause to retreat

                each into himself
                   bitter;
our other selves, our brothers—

              the likes of us.

III.

Now I recall the little Cambodian boy
with rotting teeth
at twilight
amid the flock of beggars
outside
      the frightening wat
(the dusk, the jungle sound coming on fast)
asking
      not for money
                but for a pen
so he could continue
his English
      lessons.

———————————

(*Address and Envoi*:)
      Boy,
      I hope you got your pen
      and will live
      to write well;
      that many of us will
      see each other again.

POEM

Summer dead.
Suddenly, regretfully,
leaves color
early.

Fall
sunlight is weary;
hesitates by
the magnificent forest.

Summer dead.
The wind increases,
life's transparency
smiles more faintly.

Summer dead,
still,
out of disorder
somehow the elegance.

—by Setsuko Masaoka,
    trans. with Nobuaki Sumomogi

SEARCHING

In me
you look for
an unknown sea of flowers,
extending soft breezes,
unseen forests of honey;
you look for
a pet bear without a head,
the eyes of a crippled dog;
you look for
a picturebook I know
but you don't, and the ends
of life
that I sense, but you don't.

You know the sprouting dream
—but I forget.

A variable star you know—but
I forget.

You search, and
I do too, for
a giant bird,
also lost.

—by Setsuko Masaoka,
        trans. with Nobuaki Sumomogi

A RESURRECTION

Bracken, dragon-fly and stream.
A world beyond death I conjure up.

Then! There! the great sky is
full of wonderful stories.

> But a few moments and in blue sky
> black clouds loom, loom,
> threaten to swallow the world,
> sky, sea, even I.

—by Jyunzo Sawai,
    trans. with Nobuaki Sumomogi

THE ANGRY BUILDING

The burnt, ruined building
struggles and trembles like a starling,
its wings torn off.
It nearly faints with anger.

The ancient Japanese asked mercy of the moon.
But, on the contrary, they resigned themselves
to sun and to the vices.
They were devoted. So!

Miracles don't happen now either.
Short-brained persons still ask
something about the relationship
between time and love.

The building stops drowsing;
remains angry still.
It exists yet.
Starlings exist yet.

> —by Jyunzo Sawai
>   trans. with Nobuaki Sumomogi

CONSTRUCTION I
(Higashi-Fuchu/London)

We ran
together
to the train,

Two
who had wasted
too many summers.

CONSTRUCTION II
(Shinjuku)

Love
and in the night
you say

"My father
was killed at
Hiroshima."

The wound
forever
in both of us

And love
forever
is both of us.

CONSTRUCTION III
(Higashi-Fuchu)

In the very dark night
in nearly total silence,
exactly in time,
and precisely together
two old men ride their bikes by,
silently friends
going to work, still.

I can only hope
to go into the dark
this lovely way.
Look beside the walk:
small flowers may just
be seen in the grass,
even though it's eleven.

CONSTRUCTION IV
(Kadena)

Today's
an ending.
Our petulance
grows, understanding
each other.

We hold
fresh contempt?
No, but deep the
rooting cancer is
all health.

My Love,
poems burn—each
selfish; all the
coals glow into night
or lust.

CONSTRUCTION V
(Kadena)

Heart have you
not grown
hard enough to
stay from this
morbidity, these tears
formed to all
          purpose
out of air?

CONSTRUCTION VI
(Okuma)

No smiles.   The
little boy sitting
          there.

CONSTRUCTION VII
(Kadena/London)

Season
change and hint
of promise; bud,
fruit, leaf, or snow fall,
Dear One.

Then we
think or act
in color: Green,
orange, brown-red, white;
trusting.

CONSTRUCTION VIII
(Kadena/Tokyo)

      A new
and steady burning selfishness,
like a sunflower maybe,
like a cornpatch with
tall stalks giving shade
and mystery when you're ten.
      I am not even
ashamed to puddle
in words like I
am right now, my dear.
      And this is, as you are,
totally new
tone to me.

CONSTRUCTION IX
(Tokyo)

Open a new book,
open you,
surprised
at each
chapter,
      regretting any
putting aside but
not entirely, for the
joy of taking up again.

CONSTRUCTION X
(Tokyo)

Form of a flake
in your
mind.   The love,
coming slowly down
on the word,
on the world.

U.S. OFFICERS' CLUB:
TOKYO, SUMMER

Fat and pimpled, 17,
the colonel's son
guards at the pool.

Hysterically
14, 12, 11 year-old
daughters of the general
take his Jungle Jim hat,
shades, and yell
on his bullhorn.   A few
splash into
dusk in the short and shallow pool.

It's cooling finally
in Tokyo.
One lithe Jap, hired guard,
can swim,
has a 12-hour shift
and can laugh;
shifts well on duty.
The afternoon extends.

I watch, aesthetics being my cause,
mine and the waiters,
daughters and wives.

JUXTAPOSITIONS AND NIGHT NOH
(Kyoto: for Eleanor King)

In the grave hairs
grow on heads of innocence
forever,
as the foolish, inconstant of us
try to go back
        to turtle island,
forgetting that the crane sweeps
eternal over the sand of ocean,
that the proper turtle
        is eternal
and goes ahead always
        directly in
a way of thought.

Heraclitus?
No. More positively,
indeed as Prince Hiro
at the department store,
        about four,
said to the mechanical monster,
"Don't you scare me!"
Took the monster home with him.

Important immediacies of movement,
as still /in the grave/
the hair continues
growing.

THE PELICANS

The sun sets at Muir Beach, the tide's beautiful—
breakers peaking high and aggressive,
bottles and boards rushed up, and seaweed.
Three pelicans, big as swans, in a surf ride
below the point of the mountain, from where I am.

This lovely sun! The earth tilts in your direction,
Yo-chan. And only two weeks ago,
six hours by slow train from Jingumae, from
Tokyo, we stood together at all hours at
another beach, living at the inn
you favored from last year's holiday.
        And the cool, and to sleep in such silence
after the July sun those days.
The mistress of the inn brought us cold ears of corn
after supper, because she liked us
and there was some left.
        And the night walks on the beach,
the children in yukatas, like flowers,
and small stars, the sparklers and skyrockets
and shooting candles against the night,
and a future with such room under heaven.

Too soon the express jolts to where we were
(the awful movement of away, finally away, is fast).
A matter of hours, a whole Pacific
to here. Muir Beach. Pelicans. Surf crash,
a white, scavenging dog.

73

Envoi: It is lovely here,
was lovely there
because you were.
The pelicans fly
past sight around the peak.
I wish for cranes
and turtles—and return.
Heather and Susan,
all of us, dig for things
in sand. Then
it is cold suddenly;
it is time for home.

—IV—

Strands

DIRECTION

Deafening silence
from All-Points,
personal, shakes the
intricate hand.

The traveler wonders
how long he can
stand in the unholy
roiling of market.

The fear compounds
and if he shows it
no forgiveness
can be forthcoming.

O himself the track
the weaker spoor
still's in the wind.
"Toward what ends?"

But his election
of movement was his
own election and
he knows it true.

So he hides the
intricate shaking
beneath the table
and if able smiles

about, about as
much as he dare smile
to keep from panic.

DRIVE IN THE COUNTRY

" . . . and dance a dance." —Sam Miller

    The pheasant standing
    there like a
    proper squire
    in the field
    at bright 5
    on the way to
    Summerville!

    One stands a stand,
    Sam, as hardly
    as necessary,
    as to dance is
    necessary
    and more commonly
    felt.

    As Pound points out
    in the Confucian
    sense,
    to be, properly,
    is the most important
    thing in
    any world.

(That I write this note
braced—
the paper
on the old billfold
my beloved students
made for me in Greenland
is part
of the fabric,
is the fabric.
   40 miles
   north of The Circle,
   APO 121:
   that was Sondrestrom.)

That we exist
is somehow
the comment,
and that at this moment
the Summerville Squire
stands
so important.

THE BURNING OF THE IMPERIAL
CAFE ON DEPOT STREET

Not only did the joke of a down-town
sociological center where the old whore
house was go up in smoke so

did a lot of other dreams and wild drunks
at breakfast and other dreams and the
assuagement of coffee and the necessity of

checks cashed and the plural necessities
of cheap meals; a great deal indeed of what
there was in my town went—went with the enjambment

of the reality, a harsh reality. Pasts and dreams
sent out to hope to find a new joint
to feel pretty much at home in any time,

any time of day or any day. The cigar
store went up in the same flames—over a quarter
of a city block. Worst of all the shock again

in the peculiar center of the chest, shock
telling again, "You can't stop time."
It took four hours to be able
to go to the scene with others.

LOVE POEM TO MY TOWN

We want somebody to be
silent with
and love

(Stand up at night, dark
enough to see and just about
quiet enough):

I love you, town;
what the promise has been,
with Minam, Old Joseph's, our Wallowas;

What delights Al, Joe, Jim, Bill, the
fisk! The fish! The mountain yields elatedly
"Sixteen inches, coming and going: *rainbow.*"

> Line cast,
> cold enough to keep some fat around the heart:
> I love you, Town.

NATIONAL POETRY DAY: 1965

Jarrell,
you're dead today.
I who have also
inscribed against death
stand in public
and stream tears,
and I'm supposed to read,
coherently, later today,
in Fort Smith, Arkansas,
about the good of the poetic mind—
and poetry.
But you won't leave my mind long enough.

You're gone
and Creeley was at last
with us in my home
last week, warmly alive,
wise, keen, brilliant.
In turn, we were
at Vancouver together
when word came
Roethke
has been found dead
in the water . . .
in the water.

Jarrell
Jarrell
Jarrell

CAMPUS TWO or
GARLANDING YOUR SO-FAR
(for Louis Zukofsky)

They're all back and what of it—
you knew you'd botch
it at best,
at worst screw
it up and
do yourself in
finally in the
Glorious Infinality of
the Aesthetic Grope.

     Blue Boy
     Whistler's Mother
     Sun Flarz and ears.

Another year that demands
trimming.

Spinner.
     Lure.
         Up on the
shelf with the fake butterfly.
The odd one out, catches,
but what
's a trout panned?
         Snout? Lip? Love?

  V the letter *V* is
one way or another
       to
as is even the crudest
stone knife.

CODIFICATION AFTER
MUNTZ AND WHITELOCK

A necessity of
the time
that I tell you
such that I
wound people
      not wishing
to
I tell you stand
      off from me,

———————————

like a sharp black line.

———————————

To know it you
need not be
hurt
   & friendship can run
a good course.

To hope
and fight
as one
     as the housecarls
is no less vital now.

A DAY AT THE UNIVERSITY
(Near Dusk)

Like "to a boy on a skate board
outside the anthropology building,"
this:
I suppose you are stupidly
refusing to give it
up, young man.
Just because you do it well.
And I admit you don't demand
an audience.
But OF ALL THINGS TO DO!
—You at least
seventeen.

This from The Admonisher. "What is
The Admonisher, or who," you ask, shithead?
It is
a Piaf
who can't sing, who has
pocks and
halitosis
like
myself.

O there are so many great deaths!

CARPE DIEM (AFTER PLACITAS)
(for W.D.)

What mad/ dog/ wild/ god/ riffles the cove

    the inlet/ arroyo

where was it—the bird—

where did it go how/

      did it/ come

as accident—crossing/ crossing

          in against the mountain

        in the heart/
        of the mountain—
a matter of burrow—

          —no dog
          —no flower brighter
          —no home
            sounder.

        Light beams
        crossing/ crossing.

(How funny they'd made me throw away the 3rd rate ro-
mantic Maxfield Parrish print, three weeks before, laughing

it was 'much too much on any wall,' all bad romanticism:
Algery.)

              and here,

          in the mountain draw

                it was!

                you are.

A LAST DAY IN MARCH

"A book, a bottle, a bench, a way of waiting . . . "
                                        —Abn Nuwas

1. And this kind letter that you sent to me.

2. I wanted to write you sooner, but the press, my own
limitations and the onset of an interesting, mild paranoid
withdrawal all worked together and so, two weeks after
your book arrived, I write.

3. Who got drunk
   and cried
   not intending to. (It is an end of tribute,
   the ultimate personal tribute.)
                              "Thank you.
                              Thank you."

4. We wait. Manure on a boot,
              mud on a thigh,
              blood on a gasht hand
              or calf.
              Slopt-over cream where
              separation happened,
              a sort of life-farm.
              All's one with us all.

5. The substance of love
                  too
   late in some instances,

tame in some,   too
violent in the sun
sometimes.

The substance of love, broadcast as seed, not
Voice of America, not BBC
not Radio Moscow.

Bodies to comprehend and minds and faces
without apology, to dig
without apology.

6. And you, after nine years, still
in the garden where you must be
and I love you.

FIRST LETTER

"Language has not the power to speak what
love indites:/ The soul lies buried in the
ink that writes." —John Clare

My Dear, how to begin this,
your being so far away and
time being so strange;
that what I love in you
is for its own dear sake,
this you know now.
Yet we are wise enough
to know love's pledges
turn lies often through Time and
not Intention.
What can we do but touch
tangibles and abstractions given,
memory of ocean,
memory of mountain,
rings,
pictures, photographs.
Words.
Recall that difficult parting,

tears (as your sobbing the last,
deep night awakened me
to what I hadn't known).
This, these simplicities;
whatever else may come,
your smile the counterpoint
to what I'd lost.

ABOUT THE AUTHOR

Ronald H. Bayes was born in Oregon in 1932 and lived in the town of Umapine during his public school years. He attended Eastern Oregon College, where he later taught, Colorado State College, the University of Pennsylvania (as a Woodrow Wilson Fellow), the University of British Columbia, and Trinity College, in Dublin, Ireland. He was stationed in Iceland in 1956–58 as a member of a U.S. Infantry combat team. He has lived in Japan on three occasions and has translated a book of modern Japanese verse with Yozo Shibuya and Nobuaki Sumomogi.

Rolfe Humphries, Charles Olson, and Robert Creeley are among the contemporary poets with whom Bayes has studied. His poetry has appeared in almost all the leading literary publications, and he has written a monograph of literary criticism, *John Reed & the Limits of Idealism*, nine chapbooks of poetry, two works (on Pound and Williams) for the stage, and a large volume of poetry, *History of the Turtle I-IV*.

Ron Bayes is foreign editor of *Subterraneans* (Tokyo), consulting editor of *West Coast Review* (Burnaby, Vancouver, Canada), poetry editor of *Human Voice* (Homestead, Fla.), and consultant for the National Foundation on the Arts and the Humanities.

He is at present writer-in-residence at St. Andrews College, Laurinburg, N.C., where he has been editor of the *St. Andrews Review*.